Title:Woodpecker
R.L.:1.8
PTS:0.5
TST:193308

Woodpeckers

Leo Statts

abdopublishing.com

Published by Abdo Zoom, a division of ABDO, P.O. Box 398166, Minneapolis, Minnesota 55439.

Copyright © 2018 by Abdo Consulting Group, Inc. International copyrights reserved in all countries.

No part of this book may be reproduced in any form without written permission from the publisher.

Printed in the United States of America, North Mankato, Minnesota.

092017

012018

THIS BOOK CONTAINS
RECYCLED MATERIALS

Photo Credits: iStock, Shutterstock

Production Contributors: Kenny Abdo, Jennie Forsberg, Grace Hansen, John Hansen

Design Contributors: Dorothy Toth, Neil Klinepier

Publisher's Cataloging-in-Publication Data

Names: Statts, Leo, author.

Title: Woodpeckers / by Leo Statts.

Description: Minneapolis, Minnesota: Abdo Zoom, 2018. | Series: Awesome birds |
    Includes online resource and index.

Identifiers: LCCN 2017939234 | ISBN 9781532120626 (lib.bdg.) | ISBN 9781532121746 (ebook) |
    ISBN 9781532122309 (Read-to-Me ebook)

Subjects: LCSH: Woodpeckers--Juvenile literature. | Birds--Juvenile literature.

Classification: DDC 598.72--dc23

LC record available at https://lccn.loc.gov/2017939234

Table of Contents

Woodpeckers

There are more than 200 kinds of woodpeckers. They are famous for hammering trees.

This hammering makes a drumming sound. It lets people know woodpeckers are near.

Body

Some woodpeckers are black and white. Others are brown and white.

Males have red
or yellow feathers
on their heads.

Woodpeckers have stiff tail feathers. This helps them **perch** on trees.

Habitat

Woodpeckers can be found all around the world. They often live in forests.

Woodpeckers also live in mountains and deserts.

Woodpeckers are **omnivores.**

Most woodpeckers look for food in trees. They hammer into tree bark. Then they catch **larvae** with their long, sticky tongues.

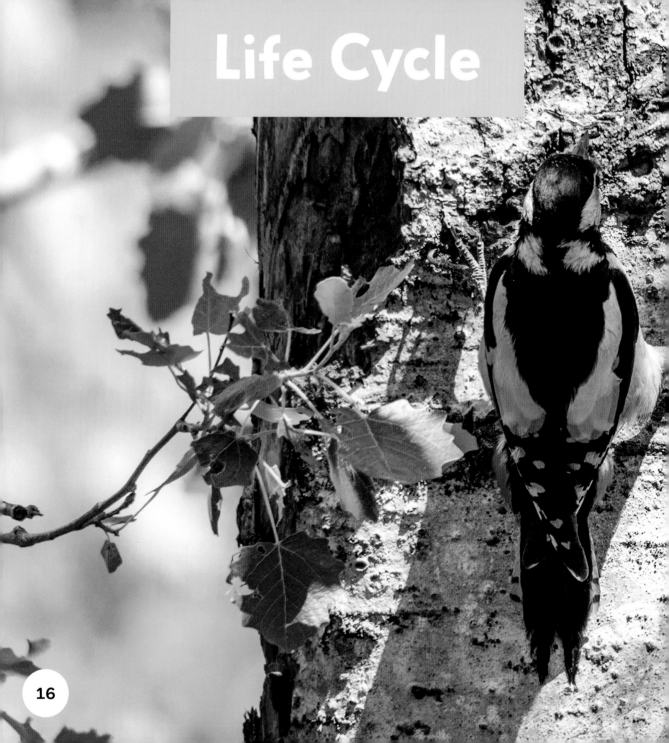

Life Cycle

Woodpeckers find **mates** in the spring.

The male and female build a **nest** together. They take turns sitting on the eggs. They keep the eggs warm. Most woodpeckers live around eight years.

Average Length

A woodpecker is longer than a basketball.

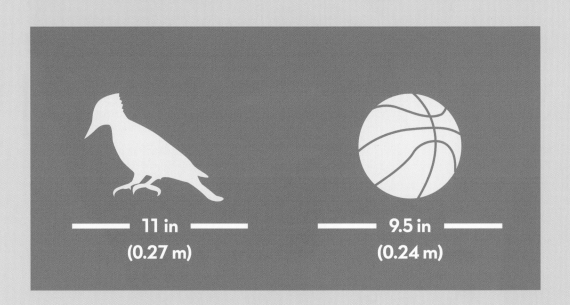

11 in
(0.27 m)

9.5 in
(0.24 m)

Average Weight

A woodpecker is lighter than four sticks of butter.

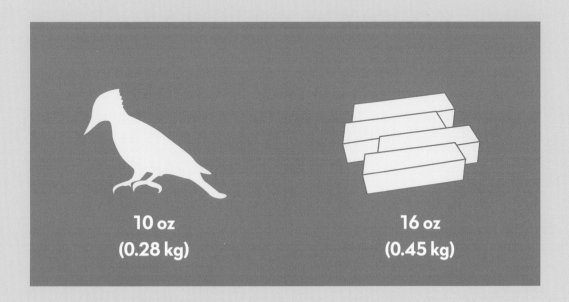

10 oz
(0.28 kg)

16 oz
(0.45 kg)

Glossary

desert – a very dry, sandy area with little plant growth.

larva – an insect in a very young form.

mates – a pair of animals who have joined together in order to have babies.

nest – a place where animals lay their eggs.

omnivore – an animal that eats both plants and animals.

perch – to rest in one place. Birds commonly perch on tree branches.

Online Resources

Booklinks
NONFICTION NETWORK
FREE! ONLINE NONFICTION RESOURCES

For more information on woodpeckers, please visit **abdobooklinks.com**

Abdo Zoom
DATABASES
BEGINNING ONLINE RESEARCH

Learn even more with the Abdo Zoom Animals database. Visit **abdozoom.com** today!

Index

color 6, 8

deserts 13

eggs 18

feathers 6, 8, 9

food 14, 15

forests 10

hammer 4, 5, 15

head 8

lifespan 18

mountains 13

nest 18

tail 9

tongue 15

trees 4, 9, 15